FOR ALL
SEASONS

"Let not your hearts
be troubled..." Jesus

Shalom,
John Winn

FOR ALL SEASONS

Prayers, Proclamations, Readings, Responses,
Planned Spontaneity, Personal Meditation
and Corporate Worship

JOHN WINN

The Preachers' Aid Society of New England
Plymouth, Massachusetts 02361

Cover design and book layout by Brenda J. Riddell.
Editing and production by Rider Green Book Publishers.

Library of Congress Control Number: 2011924497

ISBN 978-0-9819921-2-9
Paperback

ISBN 978-0-9819921-3-6
Hardcover

PUBLISHER
The Preachers' Aid Society of New England
PO Box 3386, Plymouth, MA 02360

PRINTED IN THE UNITED STATES OF AMERICA

O God,

Light the dark corners of our minds,

Warm the cold places in our hearts,

Fill the empty chambers of our spirits,

Heal the brokenness in our lives.

Amen.

Prayer by John Winn, used as the theme
for The National Conference of The Fellowship of United Methodists
in Music and Worship Arts,
July 16-20, 1989, the Claremont Colleges, Claremont, CA.

Also engraved on a stone monument in the quadrangle
at Vandebilt Catholic High School, Houma, LA.

TABLE OF CONTENTS

FOREWORD vii

PREFACE xiii

PROLOGUE xv

READING PRAYERS xix

ADVENT 3
The Advent Prayers.. 5
The Afterword 12
The Advent Proclamation...12
An Advent Prayer for Slow Walkers 14

CHRISTMASTIDE... 17
The Christmastide Prayers...19
Christmas Day 19
The First Sunday After Christmas..20
The Afterword 21
The Christmastide Proclamation 21

EPIPHANY.. 23
The Epiphany Prayers...25
The Afterword 35
The Proclamation of Purpose..35
A Meditative Reading...35

LENT 37
The Lenten Prayers 39
Ash Wednesday 39
The Gethsemane Prayers 40
Palm Sunday 45
Holy Week 46
A Reading for Good Friday 48
The Afterword 49
A Lenten Prayer for Slow Walkers 49
A Meditative Reading 51

EASTERTIDE 55
The Eastertide Prayers 57
Easter Sunday 57
Ascension Day 63
The Afterword 65
The Easter Proclamation 65
A Love Feast 66

PENTECOST 67
The Pentecost Prayers 69
Pentecost Sunday 69
The Afterword 86
The Responsive Call to Worship 86
The Proclamation of Freedom 87

MISSIONTIDE 89
The Missiontide Prayers 91
All Saints Day 99
The Afterword 106
The Proclamation of the Mission of the Church 106

EPILOGUE 109

GRATITUDE 115

ABOUT THE AUTHOR 117

FOREWORD

hose of us born in the vanguard of the Baby Boomer generation remember a requirement now long gone from most private colleges and universities: compulsory chapel attendance. We would shuffle into the college chapel (in my case Lycoming College, a small Methodist school in Williamsport, Pennsylvania) sleepy-headed, generally disinterested and just trying to stay awake during this weekly routine from which it was almost impossible to be excused. At the end we would shuffle out and other students stationed at the door would stamp our attendance cards — which had to be turned in at the end of each semester to meet the chapel requirement.

Painful as it was at the time, it is now something I look back on with appreciation. During those hours I heard some of the great spiritual and intellectual voices of the times. Among our chapel speakers were Paul Tillich, Ralph Sockman, and Norman Vincent Peale. They were the theological and pulpit giants of their day! On one occasion I had an hour-long and profound personal conversation with Paul Tillich late in the evening in my dorm lobby, where he was staying the night before chapel in the guest suite. It was about baseball!

It was the custom of our college president, D. Frederick Wertz, who later became a United Methodist bishop, to bring the pastoral prayer each week in chapel before introducing the guest preacher. The rest of the service was in the hands of the college chaplain. To the best of my recollection, President Wertz invariably set the tone for his prayer from memory with a poem by Walter Rauschenbusch — "The Little Gate to God," written in 1918 — which I can mostly recite to this day:

In the castle of my soul is a little postern gate,

Whereat, when I enter, I am in the presence of God.
In a moment, in the turning of a thought, I am where God is,
This is a fact...

When I enter into God, all life has meaning.
Without asking, I know; my desires are even now fulfilled,
My fever is gone, in the great quiet of God
My troubles are but pebbles on the road,
My joys are like the everlasting hills...

So it is when my soul steps through the postern gate
Into the presence of God.
Big things become small, and small things become great.
The near becomes far and the future is near,
The lowly and despised are shot through with glory...
God is the substance of all my resolutions;
When I am in Him, I am in the Kingdom of God
And in the Fatherland of my Soul.

Obviously, the language is that of an age before the great world wars and gender awareness, but the spirit of a profoundly anticipated connection with spiritual depths and life destiny is overwhelming! At its best, prayer is, in my mind, like a slingshot: it draws us far back and deeply close to the heart and breast of our spirit, then to release us with incredible power and insight to the ministry and mission of our life. It is the place of our nurture, growth and preparation so that interactive life becomes a joyous adventure and not an overwhelming quagmire.

Every great human spirit seems to have mastered this balance of retreat and advance; this rhythm of reflection and action; this discipline of inner healing and outbound vulnerability. The heart of every congregation is its sanctuary — a place of adoration and reflection leading to the engagement of the community with the world around it. Architecturally, we have lost much of that with the contemporary "multi-purpose" room in which we worship Sunday morning and dine that same night. It is certainly utilitarian, but seldom captures the need for a "sacred space" of quiet and retreat while listening for the "still small voice" in sacred time. For me, the notion of a "sanctuary" provides a symbolic setting for ordering the reflections and disciplines that connect me over time to concerns and powers much greater than my own narcissistic sense of the world. These impingements on my quiet times are walled out so that I can be significantly alone.

All of us recognize at some level or other our need to retreat and reflect. United States presidents have Camp David, popes have Castel Gandolfo, Wall Street tycoons have homes in the Hamptons, psychiatrists convene in Truro on Cape Cod, and those less affluent take the kids camping in the mountains! We all need, at some points in time, to get away and regroup. Recently, I helped lead a group of clergy and laity on a trip to Israel and parts of the Palestinian Authority lands. I had not been to this part of the world for about 15 years, and I was very disappointed at the crowds clamoring from dozens of tour buses at every holy site we visited. Lines were everywhere. Concession stands were built almost on top of historic and sacred sites. It was very distracting.

One evening I was complaining loudly to several colleagues about the sorry state of Holy Land tourism compared with just a decade ago. I felt that I was being pushed and shoved at every stop. One of my colleagues gave me a quasi-sympathetic smile and calmly said, "Now you have experienced why Jesus so loved the Garden of Gethsemane and the Judean desert!" We all need to step away.

This little volume is about stepping away into our prayer life. It is about the discipline of passing through that postern gate in the garden of our souls. It is so especially important for committed lay persons who dedicate their lives to discipleship, and it is absolutely essential for pastors who feel called to spiritual leadership. One of the main reasons I see for clergy burnout is their lack of discipline in watering their own souls or being in covenant with others who will hold them accountable for this. You can almost see it coming when reference to the denomination or even their own congregation is "them" instead of "we." It reminds me of a little part of the old Edwin Markham poem "...but love and I had the wit to win: we drew a circle that took him (them) in."

To me, the signs of a seasoned prayer/devotional/reflective life are as clear in the lives of those in the helping professions as the results of their work. These signs include patience, tolerance, compassion, gentleness and acceptance. They are the distinctive marks of Jesus and other epochal spiritual leaders in their dealings with everyone around them. And these marks do not constitute, but are often mistaken for, weakness rather than strength. It takes a well-grounded and centered person to confront anger, narrow mindedness, selfishness, bigotry and all other kinds of brutish behavior and not respond as though personally attacked. Inner spiritual strength is like a towering redwood that moves little in the most ferocious wind. And it enables us to lead the most ordinary persons to embrace the most extraordinary lives!

John Winn has been growing "redwoods" for a very long time. His work in leading clergy down the road to pastoral excellence has spread from Louisiana to all parts of the country. In setting up supportive growth groups for our New England pastors, we have drawn heavily from his pioneering work of combining personal spiritual journeys with an understanding of social and family systems theory. This combination brings a wholeness to our development as effective parish pastors.

The combination of being solidly grounded in your inner strength while being very aware of the family, congregational and community contexts in which your life is immersed provides a very solid foundation for holistic living as a clergy person. It is vital for keeping your creativity and your sanity in work that often tears lives apart. Throughout his life as a mentor, John has penned the prayers that have sprung from his heart. The Preachers' Aid Society of New England considers it an honor to bring these to the published page and share them across the church. We give our very special thanks to John Winn for compiling his prayers, Marcia McFee for her reflections on their meaning and context and Stephen Swecker for his editorial and production gifts and graces.

In my 45 years of active ministry, many books of and about prayer have found their way onto and off of my bookcase. Only a few remain: John Baillie's *Diary of Personal Prayer*, *The Prayers of Peter Marshall*, Rene Bideaux's *A Book of Personal Prayer*, and Ted

Loder's *Guerrillas of Grace* stand out. *For All Seasons* will now join them — especially because it speaks from the heart.

"When the heart speaks, take good notes." *

Thomas J. Gallen
Executive Director
Preachers' Aid Society of New England

* *Attributed in various sources to Judith Campbell.*

PREFACE

My friend and mentor, John Winn, has long tended to the spiritual lives of church leaders. Countless pastors have found renewed vision through his bright smiling eyes, long-hidden joy in his mischievous ways, and deep untouched yearning at his gentle invitation. Whether he is talking in front of a group about family systems, or speaking personally to you across the table, his New Orleans voice coats like a good medicine for what ails you. Yet always come the insightful questions that hit their mark and cleave clarity in the soul. More than a few times I have left the presence of John Winn simply knowing. More. About me. About life. About the Holy.

And so it is as we meet John here in these pages. We come as witnesses to his relationship with God as revealed in these written prayers. But soon we move from simply witnessing to experiencing our own lives in relationship to God. This is what John wills. He wants his prayer to turn to our prayer, and for his words to offer a jumping-off point for our words. He lures us into his depths in order for us to find our own.

Long a student of the liturgical year, I have come to believe that this rhythm of time and ritual speaks firstly to human longing. Since we became "human," we have been ritualizing our yearning — for connection with the Creator, for connection to each other. We have longed for that place, as liturgical theologian Don Saliers has said, where "human pathos meets God's ethos." Prayer is that meeting place. And the liturgical year is the context for the full range of emotions we bring before God. By offering us very personal prayers in the framework of the liturgical year, John has offered us a rhythm and ritual for our longing.

As I write this, it is the 81st anniversary of John's birth. I hear reports that he is spending it at a Tulane basketball game and then dinner with dear friends at one of the best tables in New Orleans. No doubt the chef will come out to greet him since John is beloved of pastors and chefs alike. He will eat and drink heartily just as he has always invited us to do whenever we gather around tables of earthly or spiritual food. He will expound on the delights of each morsel just as he invites us to experience life in such a way. And the conversation will turn to the next place we might eat a great meal… with the same anticipation he demonstrates whenever he invites spiritual leaders to anticipate their next passionate adventure in ministry.

Marcia McFee, Ph.D.
Professor of Liturgy and Worship Consultant
January 22, 2011

PROLOGUE

f we do it right, before prayer becomes corporate, it has to be personal. As a pastor myself, I consider the pastoral prayer as important an element in congregational worship as the sermon. This makes private prayer all the more important for my own personal times of contemplation and reflection.

It is helpful to me to read the prayers of other people as part of my own devotions. Those that seem personal, poetic, and relevant I revisit many times. It is never about finding a "resource" for later use in my own services

PERSONAL BECOMES CORPORATE

of worship. For me it is the first step in realizing that in any given moment a multitude of silent voices all over the world are being lifted in prayer. In that moment the theological explanation of the phenomena does not matter. It is the phenomena itself that matters. And I am convinced it has helped make me a more articulate person.

In addition, it adds a sense of drama to my private prayers, not unlike when Muslims all over the world, figuratively or literally, roll out their prayer mats, kneel facing Mecca, and pray.

It makes even personal prayer corporate.

In the course of reading the prayers of others, I instinctively evolved a way of internalizing elements of them. Hence, as you read my prayers please do not be limited by the language I use. Find your own words. Feel free to make them fit in your own mouth and heart. Adjust them. Rearrange them. Edit them. This will be especially helpful if you are reading them for personal meditation and spiritual formation.

POETIC FORM, SACRED PAUSE, SILENT SPACES

Purposely and for personal use I have spelled out these prayers in poetic form. I have done this to invite you to repeat a line here and there when it seems to be asking you to do so. You might even change the inflection of your voice from time to time. Let the words highlight themselves in this way. Let them internalize.

A linear, prose form often motivates us to read through rapidly, even to skim or skirt. In a poetic form one can respect spaces between sections of thought and feeling, be still for a moment, taking time for a sacred pause, then, continue again. The challenge, "what-is-this-about-in-my-life," is what pushed me to put most of the prayers in the first person. Indeed, they are my prayers. The invitation is for you, in your own way, to make them yours, too.

For example, even in the corporate saying of the Lord's Prayer I often find myself silently repeating a phrase as I pray it with the congregation — even putting it in the first person: "lead us not into temptation" becomes "lead me not into temptation;" "forgive us our trespasses" becomes "forgive me my trespasses;" "as we forgive those who trespass against us" becomes "as I forgive those who trespass against me." It is as though, subliminally, I am doing a Lectio Divina of the prayer even as I pray it. Try that with some of the prayers and readings herein.

ABOUT THE AFTERWORD

In New Orleans, where I live, "lagniappe" has special meaning. It is "a little something extra." Or, to put it another way, it is a small gift added to something already shared or purchased.

Following the prayers for each season of the Christian Year is a section I am calling "The Afterword." It is lagniappe.

An Afterword is an outgrowth of the private prayers. It is not unlike the designation, "After Service," often seen in the *Book of*

Common Prayer and adapted by John Wesley in his laboriously named, *The Sunday Service of the Methodists in North America, with other Occasional Services* (London, 1784).

In my case, The Afterword is the offer of "a little something extra" in the form of Proclamations, Readings, or Responses consistent with the season. Useful in themselves, they may also be a catalyst to your own spontaneity and sense of creativity.

During morning worship some time ago I noticed a number of children sitting on several pews around me. Some were wiggly, some were whiney, some were coloring or being otherwise occupied by material given them by a church usher, some were almost dozing off on a parent's shoulder. But then, when the minister said something like, "Let us pray the prayer that Jesus taught us, 'Our Father, who art...'" most of them changed position, became still, closed their eyes, some folded their hands, all seemed to become a part of that bit of drama.

CORPORATE BECOMES PERSONAL

Not only was I impressed that they had actually been listening, but, more so, that they sensed the scene had shifted. Something *holy* was taking place. I have noticed this again and again. If only for a moment worship had become something they did, not something that was done to them. The corporate became personal. I vowed never again to lead a service of corporate worship without including the Lord's Prayer.

Perhaps it has been a little child that has led me to this interest in the place that prayer plays in worship, personal or corporate, for all seasons of our lives. It is what informs and deepens our proclamations, readings, and responses. Prayer even draws forth from us a spontaneity that can dramatically link worship to life.

So it is we begin with Advent at the outset of the Christian Year, the birth of a very special child, who draws us into the adventure of what is yet to be.

Come and see.

READING PRAYERS

+ **READ** the prayer slowly.

+ **READ** the prayer more than once.

+ **CHANGE** the inflection of your voice
from time to time.

+ **REPEAT** a word or phrase that seems
to be asking you to do so.

+ **FEEL FREE** to change some of the words
to fit you and your life situation.

+ **LINGER OVER** the challenge:
What-is-this-about-in-my-life?

+ **GO OVER** the words and phrases that
your heart has highlighted.

+ **THINK:** "Lectio Divina."

FOR ALL SEASONS

*"Every journey has a secret
destination of which the
traveler is unaware."*
– Martin Buber

ADVENT

A time of anticipation *that One will come who knows our needs and limitations and will help us overcome them.*

THE ADVENT PRAYERS

First Sunday in Advent

O God,
I have never known you to coerce,
to punish, or to condemn,
but you *have* made me *wait*.
It was the waiting of a pregnant Mother
sensing a new birth.

You have made me *wonder*,
but it was the anticipation
of one longing for a vision
of the next great gift of love.

You have made me *cry*,
but it was the cleansing of an
inner soul too full of itself.

So, Dear God,
when next the night comes
and the wind howls,
I will remember that
waiting has been worth it,
wondering has been fulfilling,
crying has made me deeper.
In the name of the One
who is Mystery itself.
Amen.

Second Sunday in Advent

The Sacrament of The Lord's Supper
for Advent and/or Christmas Eve.

THE ADVENT PROCLAMATION

Leader:
What we do in this Season
is blessed in a very special way.
The carols we sing,
the prayers we pray,
the words we say
are not our songs or our prayers, or our words.
They are a Gift,
inspired by the Giver of All Words,
even that Word made flesh
that dwells among us.
For in this Season we proclaim, again,
the birth of Christ,
who comes to show us everything
we will ever need to know about God.

THE PRAYER OF REMEMBRANCE
AND CONSECRATION

O God of Light,
in whom there is no shadow,
your gifts flow from the beginning of time.
I am thankful for Creation, itself,
when your Spirit gave form
to the chaos of energy and matter,
and when your Word
brought forth light on the face of the earth.

Your gifts continued with ancient ancestors
I call my own,
like Noah, whom you blessed
with the colorful promise of the rainbow.

In the desert you gave gifts of manna
and living water to the weary wanderers,
whom you led by a cloud by day.

At the Red Sea and on the mountain
and with a pillar of fire by night,
you brought Moses
face to face with Truth
as he had never known it before.

I am thankful for Miriam,
who teaches me to dance in celebration;
I am thankful for Ruth and Naomi,
who showed me the value
and the resiliency of commitment.

I am thankful for the Prophets,
who preserved for all humanity,
a vision of a future
that could be new and different.

Then,
in the fullness of time,
you sent your light into the world
in the form of a newborn baby,
fragile and vulnerable,
who grew to be the very light of light,
full of grace and truth,
revealing your nature to us all.

Thanks be to you, O God.
May I receive your gifts
with joy and humility.
With this bread and wine
may I open my heart anew to receive
your love and grace in Jesus Christ.

Help me to find ways to share that
grace in loving kindness
with every life I touch,
in the name of the one we proclaim
in the mystery of faith.
Amen.

THE SHARING OF BREAD AND CUP

Read responsively.

As we give each other gifts in this season,
Let us remember that this Bread is a gift.

"Given by the One who gave us the sun and the moon and the stars and the earth with its forests and mountains and oceans and all that lives and moves upon them and within them."[1]

As we give each other gifts in this season,
Let us remember that this Cup is a gift.

"Given by the One who has given us all that grows and blossoms and bears fruit; and all that we quarrel about and all that we have misused; and to save us from our foolishness, from all our sins, God comes and dwells among us."[2]

Come now to receive these Gifts of God,
for the People of God.

Third Sunday in Advent

O God,
as Mary and Joseph went
from Nazareth to Bethlehem
and there found no room;
so Jesus went from Nazareth to Jerusalem
and was despised and rejected.

As in the poverty of a stable Jesus was born,
so by the richness of his life,
death and resurrection
are we saved.

And, dear God, as we come this day
to make room for love in our lives,
so may we also, with thankful hearts,
open ourselves to the New Beginning
we are being offered now,
in Jesus' name,
Amen.

Fourth Sunday in Advent

Dear God,
We have made the biblical journey from
Bethlehem to Jerusalem with Jesus many times.
It is so like my own journey, which has been
made easier because someone has forged
the way ahead of me.

I do not always remember
everything about the journey.
Yet, memories I could never have recalled myself
have been preserved for me in unexpected ways.
I am often given New Life
by those who remind me
of words of love that were
whispered into my ears long ago.

They make me know deep within that
the future will bring me once again
to the Center,
where all things are made New.
Amen.

THE AFTERWORD

Advent Sundays deserve a Processional to open the Service if at all possible. Things that happen in the aisle can be magical. Picture this: With the Christ Candle leading the way, unlit until Christmas Eve, the Choir processes, leading the Congregation in singing the first two stanzas of "Hail To The Lord's Anointed." The Choir stops in the aisle when the Christ Candle reaches the front of the Sanctuary. After the second stanza the congregation is led with great fervor in The Advent Proclamation. Then the third and fourth stanzas are sung, with the Choir completing the processional and the Christ Candle put in its place in the Advent Wreath. Here is how it unfolds:

THE HYMN

Hail to the Lord's Anointed, great David's greater Son!
Hail in the time appointed, his reign on earth begun!
He comes to break oppression, to set the captive free;
to take away transgression, and rule in equity.

He comes with succor speedy to those who suffer wrong;
to help the poor and needy, and bid the weak be strong;
to give them songs for sighing, their darkness turned to light,
whose souls, condemned and dying, are precious in his sight.[3]

THE ADVENT PROCLAMATION

In unison, with feeling.

"Behold, the days are coming," says the Lord, "when I will make a new covenant with my people." That great promise is happening again in this Advent season. We prepare for it with the same care that we anticipate the birth of a child, for like life, it keeps coming and never ends. We are the people who know the end of the story as well as we do the beginning. We know, in

faith, that our hope will be fulfilled; that peace will reign; that sorrow will become joy; and that our love will be met with love. Unto us a child is born, the Savior of the world, my Savior.

THE HYMN (continued)

He shall come down like showers upon the fruitful earth;
love, joy, and hope, like flowers, spring in his path to birth.
Before him, on the mountains, shall peace, the herald, go,
and righteousness, in fountains, from hill to valley flow.

To him shall prayer unceasing and daily vows ascend;
his kingdom still increasing, a kingdom without end.
The tide of time shall never his covenant remove;
his name shall stand forever; that name to us is love. [4]

Of course, one of the hymns on the First Sunday in Advent should be Charles Wesley's, "Come, Thou Long Expected Jesus." Perhaps, "Hail to the Lord's Anointed" could be used the first two Sundays of Advent and "Angels We Have Heard on High" on the last two Sundays, using a second Advent Proclamation, like this:

THE HYMN

Angels we have heard on high sweetly singing o'er the plains,
and the mountains in reply echoing their joyous strains.
Gloria, in excelsis Deo! Gloria, in excelsis Deo!

Shepherds, why this jubilee? Why your joyous strains prolong?
What the gladsome tidings be which inspire your heavenly song?
Gloria, in excelsis Deo! Gloria, in excelsis Deo! [5]

THE ADVENT PROCLAMATION

In unison, with feeling.

Something new and important is about to happen. I can feel it in the tinsel and excitement of Advent. Even through the noise and confusion of people in a rush, I can feel it coming and I know what it is. It is Love, bringing peace to our chaotic world and our crowded lives. Everything is falling into place: Sing the carols! Light the candles! See the star! Here comes hope! Here comes peace! Here comes joy! Here comes love, turning Advent into an adventure and Christmas into a new birth for us all!

THE HYMN (continued)

Come to Bethlehem and see Christ whose birth the angels sing;
come, adore on bended knee, Christ the Lord, the newborn King.
Gloria, in excelsis Deo! Gloria, in excelsis Deo!

See him a manger laid, whom the choirs of angels praise;
Mary, Joseph, lend your aid, while our hearts in love we raise.
Gloria, in excelsis Deo! Gloria, in excelsis Deo![6]

AN ADVENT PRAYER FOR SLOW WALKERS ON THE JOURNEY TO BETHLEHEM

This is an experience in kinetic worship as all walk while one person gives directions and clearly and distinctly reads the prayer aloud, slowly and with feeling, pausing when it seems appropriate. All movement is done two steps forward and one back. This works best with the Communion Table in the center and with groups of three to one hundred. Find a similar prayer on Page 49 in the Lenten section for "Slow Walkers on the Journey from Bethlehem to Jerusalem."

We begin around a Communion Table, in a single-file circle, without touching, walking two steps forward, one back.

Dear God,
We have been on this journey before with
People of Faith from Egypt to the Land of Promise;
with them again as we returned from exile
in Assyria, Babylonia, Persia,
Houston, Atlanta, New York,
Chicago, San Francisco,
and other "Far Places."

Indeed,
We have been in this procession
to Bethlehem many times before.
Somehow it is all the same journey.

We understand the pace of it, the sounds of it;
the beat of it, the rhythm of it,
the ultimate destination of it.

*Break the circle, walk randomly, without touching,
two steps forward, one back.*

But we are not all at the same place on the journey.
Advent on the calendar may not be Advent in my soul.
Some of us have no home of our own;
Our Community of Faith has scattered;
Some of us are too much separated from our families.
The storms of life have upset the order of our souls.

*Re-form the circle around the Table, hand on the shoulder of
person in front of you, moving two steps forward, one back.*

I am drawn, however, to be a part of the journey.
It is not only that I know I need the support of others;
that is too fleeting and too easily becomes simplistic.
Nor is it that I think I can help someone else by my own great faith.
That is too deceiving and self-righteous.

Tighten the circle and bring it close as possible to the Table.

It is more that I want to be as close
to Christmas as is possible,
as often as possible.
I find, O God, that when I am close
to the kind of love Christmas reveals,
I become a better person.
Indeed, I become more capable, myself, of truly loving.

And it is THAT:
my enhanced capacity to love,
as mysterious as is the gift,
that brings me back, to be near once again
to any source of the life-giving
mystery that is Christmas.

In the name of Jesus,
who brings peace to my soul,
Amen.

CHRISTMASTIDE

A time of acceptance *of the gift of love in the realization
that in each new Act of Love, everyone's love is renewed.*

THE CHRISTMASTIDE PRAYERS

Christmas Day

O God
We are thankful that you have given us
Eyes of Faith

We can look at a Star
and see a Place

We can look at a Baby
and see the Future

We can stand at the beginning
of a New Year
and see Hope

For we are the people who know
the end of the story
as well as we do the beginning
Amen.

The First Sunday After Christmas

This is often a Communion Sunday.
This prayer is inspired with that in mind.

O God,
my prayer is for you to come
and be in our midst
and you do,
at Christmas,
in the newborn Jesus,
and again in the risen Christ at Easter.
It makes my heart sing, "God is *with* us!"

By the light that Christ brings into the world,
I see myself as I really am.
It does not compare with what you called me to be.
There are times when I need forgiveness,
a New Beginning,
and you come to me again and say,
"This is my body, given for you.
This is my life, laid down for you."
That makes my heart sing, "God is *for* us!"

May this Bread and Cup
always be for me symbols that keep me
faithful on my journey from
all my Bethlehems to all my Jerusalems.
Amen.

THE AFTERWORD

THE HYMN

Go, tell it on the mountain, over the hills and everywhere;
go, tell it on the mountain, that Jesus Christ is born.
While shepherds kept their watching o'er silent flocks by night,
behold throughout the heavens there shone a holy light.
Go, tell it on the mountain, over the hills and everywhere;
go, tell it on the mountain, that Jesus Christ is born.

The shepherds feared and trembled, when lo! above the earth,
rang out the angel chorus that hailed the Savior's birth.
Go, tell it on the mountain, over the hills and everywhere;
go, tell it on the mountain, that Jesus Christ is born.[7]

THE CHRISTMASTIDE PROCLAMATION

In unison, with feeling.

It has happened! The Word has become flesh to dwell among us. Something of God's own self has become a part of life as we know it. It is Love made personal! It is Love with my name on it! Once we have known that Love we cannot go back to what we had before. It is a Love that enables us not only to see ourselves as we are, but in a fullness of being of which we rarely dream. This is the good news that we, too, are children of God!

THE HYMN (continued)

Down in a lowly manger the humble Christ was born,
and God send us salvation that blessed Christmas morn.
Go, tell it on the mountain, over the hills and everywhere;
go, tell it on the mountain, that Jesus Christ is born.[8]

Epiphany

A time of sharing *love received in a way*
that will overcome human needs and limitations.

The Epiphany Prayers

Epiphany Sunday

O God,
once you said,
"Let there be light,"
and there was, and still there is.
I turn to you in thanksgiving and praise.
In every leaf
there is the wonder of creation.
In every sunrise
there is the gift of a new day.
With every breath
I experience the miracle of living.

Slow me down soon enough
and quiet me long enough
that my awareness of you may flow
into rivers of gratitude.
Open my ears
to those who caution me
about endangering life on this planet;
to those who tell me
war is an inadequate answer.
Open my eyes
to see opportunities for positive change
and to know carelessness is a poor companion.
Open my life
to live caringly, so that my children and my children's children
may live on a balanced and bountiful earth.
And in every sunset, O God,
may I see a sunrise that brings me the gift of a new day,
in the name of the One who is the light of the world.
Amen.

First Sunday After Epiphany

Never again,
O Lord,
will I look at water
in quite the same way
as I have in the past.

There is a certain sacredness
about it now.

I remember Moses parting the Red Sea
to lead the People of Faith to freedom.
I remember Jesus calming raging waters
saying, "Peace, be still."

I remember him walking on the water,
bringing us to a deeper understanding of faith.

I remember the woman at the well,
to whom Jesus gave living water.

I remember my baptism
and I am glad.
(repeat)

In the name of the One
who has cleansed us again
and again and has given us a
New Beginning.
Amen.

Second Sunday After Epiphany

O God,
You are the One who knows the life
that is alive deep inside of me.
As for me,
my own behavior baffles me.
I do not always do what I really want to do,
even when I know in my heart what is right.
Often, I have the will to do good,
but not the power.
There is a part of me that starts out each day
seeking the good life.
Yet, at the end of the day it is sometimes difficult
for me to recognize my own self.
It is an agonizing situation, and I yearn to be
set free from all that threatens and limits me.
Show me the way out,
through Jesus Christ our Lord,
Amen.

*This prayer is indebted to the J.B. Phillips translation
of the New Testament, Romans 7:15-25.*

Third Sunday After Epiphany

When I am honest, O God, there is a battle
going on inside me.
It is a battle between past, present, and future.

There are times
when every threatening memory I have ever had
seems to rise up to be faced again.
Is it true that the only way I can turn loose of those
kind of memories is by *remembering* them?
Is it true that, in reality, remembering
is a critical step toward *forgetting*?
Forgetting, at least, in a way that old scars
are no longer a threat to New Being?

Remind me that You are the One who knows
my memories even better than I.
You are the One who loves me,
memories and all.
Amen.

Fourth Sunday After Epiphany

Dear God,
What do I do when my fragile words are inadequate
for the freight of meaning I seek?
What do I do when my prayer has no voice, no substance,
only sighs and groans and silence?
What do I do when the "earthquake, wind, and fire"
shake and sway and burn me deep within?
What do I do when the "still, small, voice"
is subdued by the loudness all around?
What do I do when there is no epiphany, no "Aha?"

I know, Dear God, I know,
you have prepared me well:
I remind myself of the truest thing I know.
I let faith take me where facts can never go.
I seek someone whose warm embrace rekindles my life.
I return to that quiet place within
where I have found answers before.

Then, I wait;
actively wait.
Thank you for meeting me there.
Amen.

Fifth Sunday After Epiphany

O Creator of all,
We have allowed ourselves to be trapped
by things we should master.
Our love of *money* turns us into puppets.
Our thirst for *power* makes us heartless.
Our hungry *pride* tempts us
to misuse and abuse others.
We can justify almost anything in the name
of a good time, which we easily convince
ourselves we have deserved.
We have fallen captive to that which
we were meant to control.
And, what is worse, we magnify our sin
by spreading the gospel of these false gods
where we have the most influence—
in our families.
Help us in our struggle to know the difference
between the gods we create
and the One who created us.
Amen.

Sixth Sunday After Epiphany

O God,
No joy exceeds the joy I know when
someone opens my life
to a new and deeper meaning,
or when someone makes possible for me
a never-before-experienced
Epiphany.

I see it now. I feel it now.
That is what was happening long ago
under the piercing light of that Star!
Something set in motion long before was being
revealed anew in an undeniable way.

I see it now. I feel it now.
An event bearing the possibility of setting
me, indeed all of us,
free from whatever limits and threatens us.
I want to tell that good news
from the highest mountain.

It is grace, irreversible grace.
There are thoughts of love and acts of love,
but none can surpass your gift of love.
When I feel inadequate for day
and fearful of night,
I cherish your gift of
grace that holds.
Amen.

Seventh Sunday After Epiphany

O God
Deep within
Where silence is touched by sight
Where soul is illuminated by light
Where wrong is changed by right
In many different ways
You get through to me
But I seldom immediately understand
It takes a moment
MOMENTOUS
And all I have always known is cubed
By that Moment
Make this such a Moment
Amen.

Eighth Sunday After Epiphany

The Isaiah Prayer
Isaiah 43:1

O God,
There have been times when I have felt
that you have called me by name.

It is a mystical moment.

No matter how difficult it is to explain,
I have learned to listen first, question later.
I listen, I tremble.
Is it really you?
Or is it merely a projection of me?

Still I listen.
More than that:
I discern.

The sound does not come from outside myself.
It seems to emanate from some hidden place within.
I think of the sound as from you,
because I receive from it a clue as
to what I must do next.
It comes cloaked more in mystery than in certitude.
It enters my hearing through my heart,
and all I can say is, "Amen."

Ninth Sunday After Epiphany

O God,
my past has taught me that I cannot be an island.
I am more like a continent.
I need other people.

My past has also shown me that
involving myself with others
can become an entanglement that limits
and embarrasses me.

When my "I" and my "We" become so enmeshed
that I cannot tell where one ends and the other begins,
I become tied in knots on the inside.
You know what this does to me, O God,
when the collision takes place
with those I love the most.

That is when I prefer to live in a velvet box.

Help me to bring together these two
seemingly contradictory personal needs.
Show me ways to be a well-defined "I"
and, at the same time,
a compassionate and caring "We."
Amen.

The Afterword

THE PROCLAMATION OF PURPOSE

We gather in worship to claim our reverence for Life.

**You have taught us to love, dear God,
By first loving us.**

You have revealed to us that every person has value.

**And we have come today to reclaim those moments
When we have believed that with all our hearts.**

A MEDITATIVE READING

Come
An Invitation

It was a simple invitation
Come
I had heard it before
It seems
From others I love and respect
Come
It all began with
Come into this world
A simple invitation
Received as a gift

Come into this family
We have been waiting

Come into this space
It will set you free

Stand
Sing
Pray
Speak

Come

Come into this life of mine
Turn off the light
Even the darkness is invitation
Come
Stay
Hold
Love

LENT

A time of personal examination *as to how
we have kept our agreement to love.*

THE LENTEN PRAYERS

Ash Wednesday

Dear God,
This night help me feel as though
I am kneeling with the saints of all ages,
who discovered that it is only through
honest confession of sin to you
that one can become more than sinner.

My eyes see beyond my innocence,
so I know that yours do.
Your mercy encourages.
Your forgiveness cleanses.
Your love saves.

May these forty days until Easter
be a season in which
I keep my promises to you,
through Christ our Savior.
Amen.

The Gethsemane Prayers

The First Sunday in Lent

Dear God,
I am full of anxious questions.
I am short on reasonable answers.
I am trapped by my own inability
to make a decision.
I am reluctant to express my feelings.
I am afraid of the consequences.
I want a guarantee that everything
will work to my benefit.
There are times when I hope that
someone will take over for me.
There are times when I know
I must do it myself.
That is when I am fearful that
I am not strong enough.
I am not wise enough.
I am not caring enough.
If it is possible,
let that cup pass from me,
but if not…
Amen.

The Gethsemane Prayers

The Second Sunday in Lent

O God,
You so love the world
that you give and give and give:
the generous gift of Life itself,
freedom of choice,
sunrise in the morning,
sunset in the evening
and all those surprises in between.
Then you give us all the time there is — eternity.

I confess that my schedule often crowds out
appreciation for these gifts and my numbness
allows me to take them for granted.
Everyday living requires
such a serious investment of my energy
that I easily neglect the grandeur
all around me.
Set me free to dance
to the rhythm of your Spirit.
Help me see that even times of sorrow and despair
often enable me to discover strength
I never knew I had.
Make me strong at the broken places.

Yet, when the dark night of the soul approaches,
if it is possible, let that cup pass from me,
but if not…
Amen.

The Gethsemane Prayers

The Third Sunday in Lent

Dear Lord,
You have shown me
what a bridge Love is across my wild rivers
of anger and my deep valleys of mistrust;
how it can tame that uncompromising beast, *Guilt*,
and its constant companion, *Anxiety*.
You have shown me how Love
warms without burning,
cools without chilling,
holds without crushing.

Whenever I may be hungry,
Love can fill my emptiness.
Whenever I may be wounded,
Love can heal.
However down I may feel,
one touch of its pleasure
can make me a saint.

There are times, though, when Love
expects more of me than I have to give.
If it is possible,
let that cup pass from me,
but if not…
Amen.

The Gethsemane Prayers

The Fourth Sunday in Lent

Dear God,
I am not always sure I know
what I want for myself.
I am surrounded by some people
who want me to be more than I am,
and others who want me to be less.

What is worse,
I have those same expectations of others.
Sometimes that makes it difficult for me
to get my head and my heart
moving in the same direction.

If it is possible,
let that cup pass from me,
but if not…
Amen.

The Gethsemane Prayers

The Fifth Sunday in Lent

O God,
There are times
when I feel hopeless and afraid.
I become confused and unsure
as to how to face the next moment.
What difference does my life make
in the midst of such a vast universe?

Sometimes the thought of my own death
stirs up feelings of doubt and uncertainty.
I feel as though I am on a treadmill,
rather than moving toward a destination.

Worst of all, in the midst of my anxiety,
I become impatient and angry with those
who mean the most to me.

If it is possible,
let that cup pass from me,
but if not…
Amen.

Palm Sunday

Dear Lord,
I, too, can feel the excitement
in the long-awaited coming of One
who can change shadows into sunlight,
despair into hope,
and even death into life.
With all inhibitions down I could
join in the parades, processionals, and testimonials
for such a One.
When I am asked, though,
to join with such a person on a march that might lead to
rejection, negation, and maybe even death,
I am not so sure.
If it is possible, let that cup pass from me,
but if not…
Amen.

Holy Week

I am convinced, Dear God,
that "all things work together."
They may clatter and clink,
groan and ache, sputter and falter,
but it seems there is a connectedness in all things,
however hidden and uncertain it may be;
and however long and patiently
we must seek before we "get it."

What I am not convinced of, O God,
is that "all things work together for *good*."
I have read that more than once in the Holy Book
and I want very much for it to be true,
but that is not always my experience.
My Honesty about this seems to be
challenging my capacity to Hope.
I do not want to surrender either.

Is the good I am longing for always
off in some future time, in some unknown place?
Is it right in front of me,
but my own ego and self are so tangled
that they cancel it out?
I work very hard at "loving God,"
as well as at loving the persons around me.
Indeed, loving the persons around me seems
to be the best way that I *can* "love God."
As a result, though, much of the time
I only feel taken for granted or even exploited.

Let me say this:
I know that all things are not possible for me.
Perhaps all I can do now is find
whatever good I can in every circumstance
that is integral to my life and

extract it, *embrace* it, and *share* it
with those I care about the most.
That will not be easy for me, Lord.
Some circumstances hurt so much
that I seem blinded to any good they may hold,
But I have been trying for a long time.

Promise me, that whenever it happens again
that all I can feel is clatter and clink,
groan and ache, sputter and falter,
that you will send me a friend
who has felt the same way at times
and who can help me find a way out and beyond —
someone like Jesus.
Amen.

A Reading for Good Friday

Trust

In an ancient book
I have read of innocents
being thrown into a lion's den.
I have learned it is so,
But I have trusted.

One whom I believe has said,
"Rain falls on the just
as well as the unjust."
I have learned it is so,
But I have trusted.

Now *this* has happened.
Still, I trust.
Yes, still I trust.

For
It is in trusting
that I am alive to the utmost,
It is in loving
that I am most fulfilled,
It is in hoping
that I live to see a better day.

The Afterword

A LENTEN PRAYER FOR SLOW WALKERS ON THE JOURNEY FROM BETHLEHEM TO JERUSALEM

This is an experience in kinetic worship as all walk while one person gives directions and clearly and distinctly reads the prayer aloud, slowly and with feeling, pausing when it seems appropriate. All movement is done two steps forward and one back. This works best with the Communion Table in the center and with groups of three to one hundred. Find a similar Prayer on page 14 in the Advent section for "Slow Walkers on the Journey to Bethlehem."

We begin around a Communion Table, in a single-file circle, without touching, walking two steps forward, one back.

Dear God,
We have been on this journey
from Bethlehem to Jerusalem many times before.
We understand the pace of it, the sounds of it,
the beat of it, the rhythm of it,
the ultimate destination of it.

Break the circle, walk randomly, without touching, two steps forward, one back.

But we are not all at the same place on the journey.
Easter on the calendar may not be Easter in my soul.
Some of us have no home of our own;
Our Community of Faith has scattered;
Some of us are too much separated from our families.
The storms of life have upset the order of our souls.

Around the Table, re-form the circle, put your hand on the shoulder of person in front of you, move two steps forward, one back.

I am drawn, however, to be a part of the journey.
It is not only that I know I need the support of others;
that is too fleeting and too easily becomes simplistic.
Nor is it that I think I can help someone else by my own great faith.
That is too deceiving and self-righteous.

Tighten the circle and bring it close as possible to the Table.

It is more that I want to be as close
to Easter as is possible,
as often as possible.
I find, O God, that when I am close
to the kind of love Easter reveals,
I become a better person.
Indeed, I become more capable, myself, of truly loving.

And it is THAT:
my enhanced capacity to love,
as mysterious as is the gift,
that brings me back, to be near once again
to any source of the life-giving
mystery that is Easter.

In the name of Jesus Christ,
who has become my Savior,
Amen.

Now serve one another Communion and Pass the Peace.

A MEDITATIVE READING FOR LENT

the hungry i

there is a part of me
the location of which i do not know
the shape of which i have no idea
a part of me that is somewhere
deep within
that is the seat of all that i am

that part of me gets hungry

when all other parts of me seem
comfortable
secure
and fulfilled
that part of me can be
yearning
uneasy
and empty

in a difficult situation
when the events of my life
or those close to me become crucial
and i have to make a statement
about what I am going to be
the first word of that statement

i

comes from that part of me
that is way down deep inside

is there a person who exists
who could not talk in this way
i doubt it

this is the way God has made us
all of us have a hungry i
and like all of our appetites
this one can become the all
demanding
consuming
appetite of life

it can become a hungry i
that devours its neighbor

yet
to be real
to be human
everyone must have an i
or end up a zero
this is the way we are made

just as God does not hold our physical hunger against us
nor does God hold this hunger against us

what God does hold against us is
when we pretend
that this is *not* the truth about ourselves

when we pretend
that there are not significant times when
we do not care about anyone
or anything else just so
the hungry i
gets filled

it is the *pretense*
not the truth about ourselves
that convicts us

only when we are able to say
yes lord that is me
i cannot throw the first stone here either
only then will we be capable of receiving
the food that overcomes all hunger
the food that is the bread of life

EASTERTIDE

A time of realization *that even in the face of crucifixion love survives, deepens, and raises us to new heights.*

The Eastertide Prayers

Easter Sunday

O God of Good Friday and Easter,
overcome my willingness to take life as it is,
rather than search out its new possibilities.
Sometimes I have been deadened by hard reality
and cold facts longer than I care to admit.

Give me back the laughter,
the enthusiasm,
the optimism,
the dreams,
that help me find something
to believe in once again.

Roll away the stone from my heart
when it becomes cold
and enable me to truly live and love once more.

Help me to see myself as you see me
and to be fully alive
to the new morning
that has broken this day,
through Jesus Christ,
who has become our Savior.
Amen.

Second Sunday of Easter

O God,
I have been an Easter Christian for too long.
I joined the procession
and shouted the Alleluias for awhile,
but now I spend too much of my time
as a bystander and observer.

Forgive me when I look down on those
first followers who abandoned
Jesus the nearer he got to the cross.
I am too much like them.

Forgive me for avoiding the crosses and
reaching for the crowns.
Show me, again, that faith can handle both.
Amen.

Third Sunday of Easter

O God of the sunrise,
How I love the sunrise, the NEW.
There is a divine beauty in the never-before-expressed.
A new day,
a newborn child,
a new friend,
a new adventure.
The list abounds and the New, like the sunrise, keeps coming,
some of it with life-changing magnitude,
some of it only a momentary surge.

O God of the sunset,
How I love the sunset, the PASSING.
There is a divine beauty in the changing shadows.
A day becoming a restful evening,
a child becoming more and more precious,
a friendship becoming unrepeatable love,
an adventure becoming a cherished memory.

Yes, Dear Lord, perhaps that is it:
always about BECOMING;
realizing that my birth was not the invention of life;
that others have come before me
and I walk in their footsteps
and always will!
Sunrise, Sunset.

In the spirit of Easter,
Amen.

Fourth Sunday of Easter

O Lord,
I am thankful for all that the past has been.
Its mixture of joy/sorrow, pain/healing,
and guilt/forgiveness
have made me who I am this day.

Whatever the night may bring,
I have learned to await the new day
that comes with the brightness of life-giving love.

However long the drought, new life comes to us
as the spring rains that water the earth.
From the altars of the past, O Lord, help us
always to take the fire and not the ashes.

In the name of the one who showed us the way
from the cross to an empty tomb
and changed sunset to sunrise.
Amen.

Fifth Sunday of Easter

Almighty God,
I confess that I have not loved
as I have been loved, nor have I given
as freely as I have received.

I have heard your call.
I have seen your way.
Your life is all around me and within me.
Yet, there have been times
when I have resisted your Spirit.
I have been slow to love.
I have forgotten how to believe.

Forgive what I have been.
Help me change who I am.
By your Holy Spirit
help me find my *true self*,
that through Jesus Christ,
I may become the person
you have called me to be.
Amen.

Sixth Sunday of Easter

Dear God,
Too often in worship I center
on my petty needs and shallow hopes
to the exclusion of much
that can strengthen my faith.

Even before the time of Jesus,
you were preparing for just such
a body of followers as the Church.
Long after I am gone,
others will come willingly
to carry the banner of truth.

Help me to see myself as part
of the People of Faith of all the ages.
May I live as though I know myself
to be a vital link from
one generation to the next
in preserving the bonds of love
that make life worth living.
Amen.

Ascension Day

O God,
I seem safely removed now
from the words Jesus said from the Cross,
"Father, into thy hands I commit my spirit,"
so, now, I can ask:
How could he have said that?

Violent things had been done to his body.
I know how long I ache and yearn for sympathy
after my body takes a hit.
Surely his mind had been pressured by
the experiences of that last week,
especially the decision-making in Gethsemane.
When my mind is under such stress, O God,
I have to unpack what it is all about
over and over again.

Can it be that his spirit, though, and ours,
is lodged somewhere deep within,
like a safe sanctuary
to which we go when body and mind
are so threatened?

Can it be that his spirit,
though surely shaken by circumstance,
was uniquely his own and in the end
he committed it anew to you,
as the One who keeps it alive forever?

Help me to see
that I, too, am body, mind, and spirit;
and that no one can take my spirit from me,
nor can it ever be destroyed.
Indeed, my spirit is a safe sanctuary,
where I meet the One who keeps it alive forever.
Amen.

Seventh Sunday of Easter

O God,
the tragedy and triumph
that is reenacted in this Season
shapes me for whatever comes my way.
While I can never forget tragedies
already experienced,
I need no longer think of them
as a limitation.

Never let me remain imprisoned
to the past, O Lord,
or cynical about the future
because of disappointments of days gone by.

Help me rise above all that.
Help me to live in the
New Morning that has broken
in this Season.
Amen.

THE AFTERWORD

THE EASTER PROCLAMATION

On Easter Sunday — and, if I had my way, all the Sundays in Eastertide — I would use the Easter Proclamation as though it is the "Easter Creed." In corporate worship say it with gusto, in unison, using the following introduction:

Leader: With the enthusiasm of a Disciple,
the heart of a Pastor,
the soul of a Priest,
and the mind of a Prophet,
let us unite in *The Easter Proclamation.*

I believe
That my life is a gift,
That it keeps coming and never ends;
That more than anything I possess or consume,
It is love alone that makes it worth living.

I believe
That I am loved:
By people near and far, young and old;
That love can be a memory;
Love can be a touch;
Love can be a word spoken in truth;
But whenever and however it happens,
It, too, comes as a gift and renews my life.

I believe
That I can love:
Myself,
People who are like me,
People who are different from me.
I can do it with my whole being —
Body, mind, and spirit.

I believe
That is what loving God is all about;
And that is precisely the way
God keeps giving life back to us.
God loves us back to life!
Again and again and again!
Amen.

A LOVE FEAST
A Call to Communion

Come to the Feast of Love,

**Where that which is broken and shared brings joy
rather than sorrow, for they point to life, not death;
and they point to a God who never convicts
without acquitting.**

We are all Children of God through faith in Christ Jesus.
For as we were baptized into Christ
We have put on Christ.
There is neither Jew nor Greek,
Slave nor Free, Male nor Female.
We are all one in Christ Jesus.
So let us be together as one Family.

**Because there is one Loaf, we, many as we are,
Are one body, for we all partake of the same Loaf.**

PENTECOST

A time of connecting *with a community that is committed to let everything they do be done in love.*

THE PENTECOST PRAYERS

Pentecost Sunday

√

O Giver of Life,
We are the People
who have heard a word we cannot unhear;
who have felt a warmth that cannot be chilled;
even a fire that will not be quenched.

It moves among us,
connecting us to one another,
despite our different languages,
our different races,
our different loyalties,
our different religions,
our different cultures.

It is a language that cleanses
like a spring shower,
and at the same time warms our hearts
in a way that bonds us as One.
And no one can stop it from happening,
for at the heart of all Creation is a Unity
we are still discovering,
which instinctively we know will save our civilization.
Let us meet at that Center,
combining all the experiences that have made us who we are,
and sharing the many ways we have
heard that word, felt that warmth, and
been illuminated by the light from that fire.
Amen.

First Sunday After Pentecost

O God of the still, small voice,
I confess that during Pentecost
I spend too much time talking about your Spirit
without opening my life to receive its many gifts.

I feel its fire burning,
but I find ways to quench its flame.
Breathe in me the fire of a Spirit
that cannot be quenched.

Fill me with a love
that pours freely from me
to others and never runs dry.

Through this Spirit of Love
raise all of us
from death itself and give us
a new heart,
a new hope,
and a new life,
through Jesus Christ our Lord.
Amen.

Second Sunday After Pentecost

O God,
I am yearning for the rushing wind of the Spirit
and a flame that warms my heart
and gives me a tongue of fire.
Wind and fire often make me fearful, though.
They can require more of me than I have to give.

Too often,
fear breeds only pious chatter.
Too often,
fear is the fire that burns.
Too often,
fear deafens me to the promptings of the Spirit.

Relieve me of pretense.
Give me ears that truly hear
and a heart that is truly open.
May I sense that the rushing wind of your Spirit
comes on wings of love;
that its fire warms without burning;
that it can give me a new heart,
a new hope,
and a new life;
that these dry bones can live anew;
that the wind and fire of your Spirit
can raise all of us up from death itself,
through Christ our Lord,
Amen.

Third Sunday After Pentecost

O God,
I do not know how to pray as I should.
Help me to replace worn-out phrases
with feelings that run deep
and truly express who and where I am
in that particular moment.

Forgive me when my prayers become
an exercise or a duty
or a way of shielding myself from reality.

Forgive me when I am overcome
by a desire to hide myself from life;
rather, help me to find myself within it.

May I not vainly seek tasks more
suited to my strength,
but strength more suited to my tasks.

And please, Lord,
be patient with me when I panic
in the presence of silence.
May I learn to listen more and better.

Help me to hear the truth not only in the
"earthquake, wind, and fire,"
but also in the "still, small voice."
Amen.

Fourth Sunday After Pentecost

O God,
There is a part of me
that only you and I know about.
Sometimes I find it difficult to
share what I am feeling with anyone.

But you know what I need to say
even when I cannot find the words.
You know me better than I know me.
You know the hidden depths
and the strong yearnings.

Even when I look bad to everyone else,
you know what I am going through
on the inside.
And, what is more,
you save me from
the awful experience
of judging myself.
Thank you
for your love and forgiveness
that show me how
to give myself a second chance.
Amen.

Fifth Sunday After Pentecost

O God,
too much of my life is consumed in hostility.
Yet, I am not comfortable with hate,
not my own or anyone else's.
I am learning that I cannot hate someone else
without loving myself less.

You have shown me how love
always wins and never loses,
always finds and never loses,
always saves and never loses.

Show me again how love can break through
any barrier, dissolve hate, and bring even
the lion and the lamb within me together.

Teach me to make love, all kinds,
and not hate, any kind.
In memory of the one
whose name is Love,
Amen.

Sixth Sunday After Pentecost

Inspired by Psalm 121

Who, but you, O God,
could create the mountains?
Sometimes the majesty of them alone
lifts my spirits.

Yet, through the years, though, I have learned
that mountains have peaks and valleys.
Whenever I ignore that truth,
seemingly level places become
so rugged and steep
I cannot surmount them alone.

Through the years, also, O God,
I have learned that it is precisely
in the ruggedness and steepness
that I encounter Truth.
There are others along the way
who often help.
To my astonishment I sometimes help them.

Little by little, O Lord, I am learning
that it is my struggle with the mountain
that brings me to trust.
Help me to see these high places and low valleys
as symbols of hard-fought battles
and life-saving victories,
from this time and forevermore.
Amen.

Seventh Sunday After Pentecost

Dear God,
there are times when I want to shout
to you the name of a loved one
in need of your presence and healing.
Indeed, I sometimes say the name aloud
when asked about my concerns
in a community in worship.
Caring sometimes moves me in that way.

There are other times, O God,
when I can only hold the name
close in my heart.
I do not really know why
the silence seems more appropriate,
except that I do not want
to call attention to *my caring*
in any way that would compromise
my prayer and concern.

I rest in the assurance that you know
the name, the need, the prayer,
even before words give them wings.
The fact is, often, I do not have words,
only sighs and groans.
But you know.

The knowledge that you have knowledge
of my dear friend's unutterable need
and my own heaviness of heart
is enough.
Amen.

Eighth Sunday After Pentecost

O Lord,
I want to be a part of your
People of Faith,
but I have not always been
faithful about that.
I do not always gather with a
worshipping community
to actually *worship*.

Sometimes, driven by *fear*, I am there
to hide from what life is demanding of me.
Sometimes, driven by *selfishness*, I am there
to make sure my future will be secure.
Sometime, driven by *habit*,
I am not sure why I am there.

But I *do* know better, O Lord,
and sometimes, driven by love,
I am wholly present to express
my gratitude
for the gift of continued life
and to be as near as I can get
to that love that will not let me go.

Forgive me when I am
narrow in my faith,
shallow in my hope,
and limited in my love.
In Jesus' name,
Amen.

Ninth Sunday After Pentecost

O God,
I do not want to miss anything.
The onrush of time fills my days.
There are not enough
minutes for the hours,
hours for the days,
or days for the weeks.

I have known what it means
to live and love life,
but sometimes others
find things that I miss.

They see things to which I am blind;
hear things to which I am deaf;
feel things to which I am insensitive.

Forgive me
when my jealousy scorns them or
when I destroy them and myself
by wanting them to be me,
and me, them.

Show me how to celebrate The Now
which you have given me
for my very own.
Amen.

Tenth Sunday After Pentecost

Dear God,
words of Jesus from the Cross
keep haunting me:
"Forgive them, for they know not what they do."
It seems to me, O Lord,
that "they" knew exactly what they were doing.

And I must confess,
most of the time
I know exactly what *I* am doing.
Sometimes I feign ignorance;
or that the "end justifies the means;"
or that I did not have enough data;
or that I have earned the right to do wrong;
or that the sunshine is on the other side of the road.

I seem to need forgiveness most when
my actions die the death
of a thousand qualifications.
When I allow the hidden impulses
to gain control over me,
who better to see the depths
of who I really am, O God, than you?
That word from the Cross comes from you.
I am the one who needs to hear it,
through Christ my Savior,
Amen.

Eleventh Sunday After Pentecost

Dear Lord,
there is something within me
that I want to give to someone I love.
I cannot always define what that something is,
but to be able to give in this way
is the heart of life itself for me.

Yet,
what about *receiving*, Lord?
I get so wrapped-up
in what I think I have to give
that there are times when
I am blind to love given *to* me.
I do not ever want to block love
when it comes my way,
whatever form it takes.
Help me with my
giving
and
receiving.
Amen.

Twelfth Sunday After Pentecost

Inspired by Psalm 23:1

The truth about me, O God,
is that I have many *wants.*

Some are simple:
I *want* to be able to ride a bike.
I *want* to be able to hike in the mountains,
I *want* to be able to skate on ice.
I *want* to be taller.

Some are less playful, more complex:
I *want* more insight in all things.
I *want* peace on earth.
I *want* my children and grandchildren,
to always feel fulfilled.
I *want* to be able to live the life
that is alive inside me.

I can get bogged down in both
the playful and the serious.
I do *not* want to do that.

I have prayed for all of those things,
and more.
You have given me LIFE,
and more.
I *want* to always remember that,
and be thankful.
Amen.

Thirteenth Sunday After Pentecost

O God,
there are so many things I want to try, but do not.
Sometimes, I feel limited by my *fear* and I remain
in the little box someone else has created for me.
Sometimes, I feel that my *abilities* are limited
and that I am destined never to improve.
Sometimes, I feel limited by my *age*.
Is there too much time left or too little?
I do want to do something worthwhile with my life.
Help me to know the difference between
a right and a privilege;
an obligation and a responsibility;
a temptation and an opportunity.
May I know my parameters so well
that I can grow because of them.
It would make me more *compleat*.
In the name of Jesus,
Amen.

Fourteenth Sunday After Pentecost

Inspired by Psalm 95:1-7

O My God,
I confess it:
A joyful noise
is *not* what always comes forth from me.
Instead of praise,
what comes forth are whimperings,
groanings, discordant complaints.

And what is more,
I do not always come into your presence
with thanksgiving.
I usually have a long list of things
that need to change,
immediately.

How did I lose control of things?
How did YOU lose control of things?

All the while I know in my heart
that you are worthy of joyful noise,
even praise, and certainly thanksgiving.
But what's in it for me?

Then, in walks Luke,
with his viola,
Olin, the drummer,
Sarah, with her sweet voice,
and Noah, with his tambourine.
Grandchildren, all!

And here come their Aunts and Uncles,
my children, grown, my very own.
There IS a joyful noise
and there is praise and thankgiving,
and things HAVE changed.

Strange,
how grace works.
Amen.

Fifteenth Sunday After Pentecost

The Jeremiah Prayer
Jeremiah 18:1-4

O God,
in my heart, I know
that you have created me for
companionship:
with you and with others.
There are times, though,
when I hide from the former
and run from the latter.

Please, O God,
when I erect an imaginary wall
around myself,
show me again that I am
an unfinished creation.

In those times when I shrink
before an unwanted chasm of reality,
remind me that I live in an
unfinished world.

When seemingly unsolvable disagreements
push me into an uncomfortable rigidity,
teach me that I am clay
and by your grace
I can be re-shaped into oneness
with another unlike anything
I have ever known before.

So may I be grasped again by the
mysterious interplay between
freedom and responsibility:
you, the potter;
me, the clay.
Amen.

THE AFTERWORD

In corporate worship, the Sundays of Pentecost should begin with a well-paced, rousing hymn, which could be followed with a Responsive Call to Worship like this one:

THE RESPONSIVE CALL TO WORSHIP

This is a New Day.
And we are a New People.

If we listen carefully we can sense
the rushing wind of the spirit,

**That warms our hearts and
Gives us tongues of fire!**

THE PROCLAMATION OF FREEDOM

An important secular holiday comes during the Pentecost Season: Independence Day, the Fourth of July. Why not a "Proclamation of Freedom" made up of a blending of Galatians 5 and the Declaration of Independence? It would be spoken enthusiastically in unison and could come after the singing of the opening hymn while people are standing or at some other suitable part of the Service. Try this:

We plant our feet firmly within the freedom that Christ has won for us and will not let ourselves be caught again in the shackles of slavery. We hold these truths to be self-evident: that all are created equal; that all are called to freedom; that all are held accountable; that liberty does not provide an opening for self-indulgence. We are all endowed with certain inalienable rights, among which are life, liberty, and the pursuit of happiness. To secure these rights governments are instituted, drawing their just powers from the consent of the governed. However, if we use our freedom to bite and devour one another, let us take heed that we are not consumed by one another. We have been made free in order to serve each other in love.

MISSIONTIDE

A time for deepening *our understanding of what it means to walk by faith and not by sight.*

THE MISSIONTIDE PRAYERS

First Sunday in Missiontide

O God,
Sometimes I like my own little world too much,
especially when I act as though I am the only person in it.
I am not sure I want "Thy Kingdom to come," if it means
mine has to change too much.

Yet, I know that I cannot remain the same always,
and I do not want everyone around me
to remain the same either.
I want to grow as a person
and I want those I care about the most to grow, too.

Inform my values,
broaden my concerns,
strengthen my spirit,
deepen my dedication.
Help me to become a better person.
Amen.

Second Sunday in Missiontide

O God,
I want to live in a way that makes me alive to
everything around me and within me.
I have tasted the kind of death that comes
from being surrounded by insensitive, "dead" people.

What is worse, I have tasted the death that comes
when I have been insensitive to all that is alive around me.
I do not want to be a walking corpse,
dead before my day.
Help me to do more than merely *exist*.

Help me to fully *live* the life you have given me,
so that when physical death does come
it will not be The End,
but a New Beginning,
through Christ our Lord.
Amen.

Third Sunday in Missiontide

Dear God,
You have come to claim your people in many ways:
You led us out of bondage into the Promised Land;
You gave us commandments to help us shape our lives;
You were present in the throbbing words of the prophets;
And you came to us as a person in Jesus of Nazareth.

We confess, though, that we do not always
recognize you when you come.
We sometimes prefer bondage, when it shelters us
from having to make our own decisions.

We ignore your commandments,
thinking they are merely mortal words.

We turn deaf ears to your prophets,
preferring teachers who suit our own likings.
And we are like those on the Road to Emmaus,
who did not even know Jesus was with them.

Give us eyes of faith that see beyond
the many faces you wear
when you come to claim us.
In the name of Jesus,
Amen.

Fourth Sunday in Missiontide

Inspired by Psalm 19:1-4; 13-14

O God,
All my senses experience a feast
when they truly are aware
of the magnificence
of earth and sky and sea and air.
Even though your creation utters no words,
it makes a new statement to me everyday.
Each night comes reminding me of all
there is yet to see, touch, feel, know, believe.

With so much that is right
in the natural world all around me,
I want to be honest
about what is going on within me.

Help me, O God, to see my hidden faults.
Forgive me when I think
more highly of myself than I should.

And, above all,
keep me innocent of abusing
your creation and your people
and, especially, your children,
with my careless deeds
and my thoughtless words.

Indeed,
May my every word, yea, even
my every thought,
be acceptable to you, O Lord.
Amen.

Fifth Sunday in Missiontide

O God of nations and Lord of history,
I have been shaped by a multitude
of social mores and sacred traditions.
Some of them are religious.
Some are secular.
Some are even political.

I yearn to stay in touch with the
Prophets of Israel and
the Carpenter from Galilee.
"Let it Be" speaks to me, as do the
blues and the classics.
Two Abrahams have a hold on me:
one a Patriarch, the other a President.
I can sense a connection between
Calvary and Gettysburg.

Help me to play a part in creating a bond
between *faith and citizenship, love and justice,*
the *artistic and the religious.*
May that bond be covenantal in nature,
spiritual in its depth.

Whenever I wander from that mission
draw me back, O Lord.
Help me see how our survival as a
healthy society depends on it.

In the name of the one who says,
"I am the Way, the Truth, and the Life."
Amen.

Sixth Sunday in Missiontide

Dear God,
too often I see the circumstances
surrounding my life as a burden,
rather than as a possible pathway
to a new and different future.

Circumstances become detours.
I allow myself to get bogged-down
in problems and heartaches.
I wander in the wilderness without a compass.
I want to give this whole world
my life, even, back to you.
You created it, you can have it!
Feeling overwhelmed
can make mere humans act like that.

But you keep giving the world, my life, back to me.
You do not magically make the circumstances go away.
I have to take responsibility for them myself.
And when I do,
if I am patient enough,
thoughtful enough,
loving enough,
I will begin to see a pathway,
a crack in the door that once seemed closed,
and hear a voice in the ear of my heart saying,
"Come unto me."
And I press on...
Amen.

Seventh Sunday in Missiontide

The Bartimaeus Prayer
Mark 10:46-52

O Lord,
I have been in the darkness too long,
unable to see the light,
incapable of finding the way.
The darkness
has blinded me and made me
timid of heart,
weak of spirit,
and lonely of soul.

In that darkness I have lost my insights,
nursed my sorrows,
and honed my grudges.

Jar my memory,
open my eyes,
loosen my tongue.
Give me confidence to share out of the
depths of who I really am.

When the time comes that I can see
the Truth in love and clarity,
grant me the courage to DO it,
in Jesus' name.
Amen.

Eighth Sunday in Missiontide

Inspired by Psalm 27

To be honest about it, O Lord,
there are times when I am afraid.
There are times when I would like
to run and hide where no one could find me.
I would like to find a place
where there are not so many demands,
where all is well,
where there really is peace on earth.
There seems to be more to do and overcome
than I can manage.

Teach me your way, O Lord.
Restore my confidence.
Convince me you will be my light and guide.
Then, I would have nothing to fear.
Give my heart courage
that I may be strong
and wait for you
in the land of the living.
Amen.

All Saints Day

O God,
like a cloud of witnesses,
saints of every shape and hue
have warmed us
with your grace and all it means.

We can call many of them by name.
Miriam dances by,
spreading the joy of small victories;
Isaiah inspires our hope
for a new and different future;
Jeremiah revives our soul
by writing on our hearts once more;
Ruth and Naomi show us how to dig deeper
in our commitments to love;
Paul gently whispers again,
"We walk by faith and not by sight;"
there is Luther standing firm;
John Wesley warming our hearts;
Bonhoeffer reminding us of
the cost of discipleship.

They never leave us
and by your grace, O God,
you give us eyes of faith to see others
in that great cloud of witnesses.

There are some alive and among us, even now,
weaving themselves in and out of our lives
when grace needs replenishing
and love is the only way it can come.
Some of them even call us by name,
and whether deserved or not,
enable us to feel
that these bones can live again.
In the name of all the saints,
Amen.

Ninth Sunday in Missiontide

Day by day, O God, I meet people
who have great joys to share.
I want to feel the electricity of their joy
and acquire some of the energy that drives it.

Day by day, too, I meet people
with patient hearts, who have unfulfilled hopes.
I want to share their anticipation
and draw hope for myself
from their patience.

And day by day I meet people
with *impatient* hearts and
unfulfilled hopes — a difficult combination.
May they see in someone they trust,
a friend who has been there, too,
and has survived to say
that despite the empty spaces,
life finds a way to get better
in often unexpected ways.

When such a day comes for me, O God,
may I thank you in a clear voice
for every ounce of love you send my way.
Forgive me when I deny the ounce because
I think I deserve a pound.

Remind me that love is not measured in that way.
Whatever the quantity,
its quality is always sufficient to renew my soul
and to make it possible for me
to love more and better.

In gratitude to the One whose name is Love,
Amen.

Tenth Sunday in Missiontide

O God,
Take my formless words,
with all their jumbled meanings,
and breathe into them insight.

Take all my
commas,
colons,
exclamation points,
and question marks,
and breathe into them intelligence.

Take my wordless prayers,
the sighs and groanings,
and transform them into an
Act of Grace.

Take me, O God,
for whom the bell tolls,
and bring me to Newness of Life,
NOW
before the bell tolls.
Amen.

Eleventh Sunday in Missiontide

O God,
I like to think of myself as a modern person
and a progressive thinker, but I am often afraid of change.

I believe that the mission of the
Christian movement is to transform the world:
to enable all people to live the fullest life possible to them.
I believe *that* is the seemingly
"*impossible possible*" that God in Christ
is calling us to help happen.

That will require change, a lot of change.
Yet, too often in my own insecurity
I merely protect the status quo,
sometimes without actually realizing it.

What can stay the same? What has to change?
Remind me, O Lord, that
growth, deepening, maturing,
always requires change;
and that I can continue
to grow, deepen, and mature
no matter how old I become.

I want to live the fullest life possible to *me*, O Lord;
so keep me open to creative change.
Then, perhaps, I will be more capable
of taking on the world.
Amen.

Twelfth Sunday in Missiontide

Dear God,
I am still having trouble with
right and wrong.
Sometimes I am certain I am doing
the right thing and I get wrong results.
Other times it is obvious to me
that I am doing the wrong thing,
but I get positive results.

Learning that everything is relative
has made it even more difficult.
Collecting data, opinions, taking polls,
even reading the Bible,
all add to the confusion.

Sometimes I find myself concealing
what I know to be true,
in order to make possible a greater good.
Surely you know, O God, how I struggle with that.
I want to be your obedient child.

Please, please, never tire of reminding me
that it is not what I do that is right and good,
that makes me your blessed child,
but the fact that I am, indeed, your blessed child
that makes me yearn to do what is right and good.
Whisper it to me again, as
Brother Martin did long ago,
"The tree bears the fruit and not the fruit the tree."
Amen.

Thirteenth Sunday in Missiontide

O Lord of all history,
even as I come ever closer
to the end of the liturgical year
still
I am haunted by the words
of Jesus from the Cross:
"My God, my God, why hast thou forsaken me?"
He had at least as much reason
as the Psalmist to ask that question.
Why? Indeed, why?

How many times
have I wondered the same thing
and about much less threatening tragedies?
So much that happens to any of us
lacks a clear cause and effect correlation.
Sometimes I feel I will remain stuck
on the "Why question" forever.
Even with "forever" I do not have time for that.

I am slowly learning the more important question:
"What, now, is expected of me?
What must I do next?"
Grant me the courage, Lord,
to work through that question.
That is what this prayer is about:
Courage.
That is where Jesus found his answer
and so will I.
In his name,
Amen.

Fourteenth Sunday in Missiontide

Eternal God,
somewhere deep within
I know that endings and beginnings,
seasons and times
are safe in your hands.

For tasks I have actually completed
and for what I have learned
from the joys and pains woven
into the fabric of years gone by,
I give you thanks.

Show me how to let go of old obligations
in order to be free
for new activities and associations.
Show me how to let go of my
fears and uncertainties about the future.
Bring me to a place within myself
of quiet confidence.

May each new day be received as a gift,
as I experience more deeply
the value of life
and the sacredness of each moment.
Amen.

THE AFTERWORD

THE CALL TO WORSHIP

The Kingdom of God is like
a grain of mustard seed, small, when sown,
but grows to become the greatest of shrubs.

So may it be with us.
May the seed of faith within us
Grow into many acts of love.
Amen.

THE PROCLAMATION OF THE
MISSION OF THE CHURCH

In unison.

We are the people…
Who have heard God's "yes" to our lives,
Who have received "grace upon grace"
As wave after wave of God's love claims us.
We are the people of God, the Church,
Who have said "yes" to God's "yes,"
Who have seen that saving Word in Jesus Christ;
Who have felt that heartwarming embrace
In the Holy Spirit.

We are the people…
Who remember our mothers and fathers in the faith,
Who crossed the Red Sea,
Triumphed over the cross,
And found a way to say
This grace-filled "yes," even to us.

We are the people of God, the Church,
Who understand that this memory is in our hands
To preserve and pass on to generations unborn,
Not merely in words and ritual,
But in the willingness
To lay down our lives for each other.

We are the people...
Who confess that we have often
Seen our own needs first,
Been deaf to the painful cries of the oppressed,
Tasted and preferred the sweet security
Of our own sanctuaries to the
Bitter winds of the outside world,
And are afraid to touch the hurts of others
For fear that they might be contagious.

We are the people of God, the Church,
Imperfect, but changing,
Unwise, but learning,
Incomplete, but growing.

We are the people...
Who have heard a word we cannot unhear,
Seen a Savior we cannot unsee,
Heard a promise we cannot forget;
We are the people of God, the Church,
And we know in our hearts
That salvation and service are inseparable,
That our mission is to the world,
In the world, but not of the world,
And that we will not fail.

And so the cycle of all seasons comes to an end ...
... No, I think it simply begins anew,
again and again.

*"Every journey has a secret
destination of which the
traveler is unaware."*
– Martin Buber

EPILOGUE

t is worth repeating: Worship is something we do. It is not something that is done to us. Nowhere is this more evident than in that private act of worship we call *prayer*. When worship is truly worship, we are drawn into it as into a gripping drama. Likewise, when prayer is truly prayer, we are lured deeper and deeper in the direction of who we really are. It is also relational. All prayer is dialogical.

PRAYER AS DRAMA

In worship — and in prayer, as in life — there are no mere theater-goers present. We are not the spectators. *God* is. God is the one watching. Thanks to Soren Kierkegaard's fertile mind for that "theater-goers" thought.[9] Whatever we mean when we say "God" in prayer, it is to that experience toward which we are being lured, deeper and deeper.

For All Seasons is, indeed, a venture into the seasons of our lives; an effort to lure us deeper and deeper within, and to enhance the sense of drama that makes one's own personal meditations memorable. The word "drama" itself dates back to the early 16th-century Greek, which has as one definition, "any situation or series of events having vivid, emotional, conflicting, or striking interest or results." I will take that as a significant aspect of worship, private *or* corporate.

Though I consider myself non-theist, many of these prayers may seem to be in a theistic mode. By non-theist I mean that I do not expect some day in this life or another to be ushered into a room and introduced to God, sitting on a throne or behind a desk, or at an impressive computer.

However, the power of myth still has a hold on me. It seems to me that in a mysterious way some of the mythological language communicates better than any language I can devise. I find it more satisfying to begin a prayer with "Dear God," or "O God," than with "O Process of the Universe...," or something like that.

THE NAME WE GIVE AN EXPERIENCE

I think of God as the name we give an experience. It is not just *any* experience or event, but one that has been life defining, life changing, life sustaining, life renewing. In the midst of those kinds of experiences I realize that there is always something *more* going on than what I can do myself, or even the sum total of what all of us can do.

It seems to me that this is the central point of any world religion. It is about deep speaking to deep. Whenever deep speaks to deep, Grace happens. In that moment, we become connected to the Source of life in a unique and mystical way.

God is an "Up-Againstness," an event that can happen anywhere, in many different ways, and is often cloaked in surprise. Like Moses and the fire that would not be quenched, or Jeremiah feeling that the truest thing he knew about life was not written on stone, but on his heart, or Jesus in Gethsemane, or Mary Magdalene at the Empty Tomb, or the early disciples at Pentecost, or *me* coming to my senses after heart by-pass surgery. Make your own list.

To one degree or another I think more people than we realize (and more so than *they* actually realize) translate meanings into the non-theistic in their inner journey toward the numinous — whatever form, shape, or process it might inhabit. This immediate and spontaneous translation of the theistic into the non-theistic makes prayer and meditation, for me, more than an inner conversation with myself. It enables me to value a dialogue with the something More that is going on in and around me.

Maybe Robert Frost gets closest to it, after all:

We dance round in a ring and suppose,
But the Secret sits in the middle and knows.[10]

Somehow, the knowledge that God has knowledge of me is enough.

ENDNOTES

1. Attributed to Sigrid Undset, Norwegian novelist, 1882-1949 (born in Denmark, lived mostly in Norway). In 1924 she converted to Roman Catholicism and became a lay Dominican. In 1928 she was the first woman to receive the Nobel Prize in Literature.
2. *ibid.*
3. James Montgomery, 1821 (based on Psalm 72).
4. *ibid.*
5. Traditional French carol, translated by James Chadwick, 1862 (based on Luke 2:6-20).
6. *ibid.*
7. John W. Work, Jr., 1907 (based on Luke 2:8-20).
8. *ibid.*
9. *Parables of Kierkegaard*, edited by Thomas C. Oden (Princeton University Press, 1978), pp. 89-90 (excerpted from *Purity of Heart Is to Will One Thing* by Søren Kierkegaard, pp. 180-81, SV XI 114-115).
10. Robert Frost, "The Secret Sits" from *A Witness Tree*. New York: Henry Holt, 1942.

GRATITUDE

eep gratitude to Thomas Gallen and the Preachers' Aid Society of New England for their willingness to publish *For All Seasons*; to Cathy MacGovern of Preachers' Aid for the initial contact and encouragement; and to Stephen Swecker for his guidance in the editing and publishing process.

Special gratitude to my favorite preachers, who surround me with grace: my wife, Carole Cotton Winn, Director of the Academy for Spiritual Leadership; my daughters, Callie Winn Crawford, Senior Pastor, Rayne Memorial United Methodist Church, New Orleans, LA and Lane Cotton Winn, Associate Pastor, Aldersgate United Methodist Church, Slidell, LA. None of this would be possible without the help of my three sons, Johnny, Dan, and Mark, who have excelled in keeping me adequately supplied with oyster po' boys.

And there is no way to measure the gratitude for my indefatigable editor, copy reader and computer guru, Marilyn Hebert, the "Queen of Commas."

ABOUT THE AUTHOR

"More retired" rather than "less retired," John Winn has resumed one of his first loves: writing. The prayers included in *For All Seasons* come naturally for him, having served as a pastor, consultant and mentor in the Louisiana Conference of The United Methodist Church for more than five decades. He lives where his roots are, in his beloved New Orleans, with his wife, Carole, who also is a United Methodist pastor. There are five children, two of whom are ordained, four grandchildren — and lots of friends. John is a graduate of Tulane University and Perkins School of Theology at Southern Methodist University. He also was awarded a Doctor of Divinity degree by Centenary College.

To contact John about this book, you may send him an email at *johnwinn@forallseasons.info*. He also invites visitors to his web site: *http://johnwinn.squarespace.com*.

To order additional copies
of this book, visit
WWW.FORALLSEASONS.INFO